ANIMAL MIGRATION

by Janet McDonnell

Created by
THE CHILD'S WORLD

Distributed by CHILDRENS PRESS®
Chicago, Illinois

The publisher wishes to thank the following for the use of their drawings and photographs: Lincoln Brower, 25; Jerry Hennen, 13; (John Hicks)/Australasian Nature Transparencies, 17; Karen Jacobsen, 19; T.E.S. Langton, 15; F. Lanting, 45; Thomas D. Mangelsen/Images of Nature, 41; James P. Rowan, 35; Leonard Lee Rue III, 9; Ron Sanford, cover, 5, 7, 21, 29, 31, 39, 47; State of Alaska Division of Tourism, 11; (F.S. Todd)/VIREO, 37; Tom J. Ulrich, 23, 43; Wide World Photos, 27.
(Thank you also to Steven D. Sanders of the Prairie Creek Fish Hatchery for taking the photo on page 33 for The Child's World.)
cover design by Kathryn Schoenick

Library of Congress Cataloging-in-Publication Data

McDonnell, Janet, 1962-
  Animal migration / by Janet McDonnell.
    p. cm. — (Amazing animal facts)
  Includes index.
  Summary: Examines the migration habits of such animals as the caribou, red crab, ruby-throated humming-bird, and gray whale.
  ISBN 0-89565-514-4
  1. Animal migration—Juvenile literature.
[1. Animals—Migration.] I. Title. II. Series.
QL754.M38   1989
591.52'5—dc19   88-36640 CIP AC

CHILDRENS PRESS HARDCOVER
EDITION   ISBN 0-516-06389-8

CHILDRENS PRESS PAPERBACK
EDITION   ISBN 0-516-46389-6

1 2 3 4 5 6 7 8 9 10 11 12 R 97 96 95 94 93 92 91 90 89

ANIMAL MIGRATION

Grateful appreciation is expressed to Mark Rosenthal, curator for the Lincoln Park Zoo, Chicago for his assistance in insuring the accuracy of this book.

If you've ever watched the skies in the fall, you've probably seen one—a huge, dotted V moving across the sky. What you saw was a flock of geese flying south for the winter. And geese aren't the only animals to take such a trip. All over the world, animals are on the move. Their seasonal trips are called migration. Some animals migrate thousands of miles to the same place every year. Most face terrible dangers throughout their trips.

Why do they do it? The simple answer is that animals migrate to stay alive. They may travel to a warmer place, a place with more food, or a safer place to have their babies.

But long ago, people didn't know why certain animals left them every year. And they had no way of knowing where the animals went. Many people once thought that cuckoos turned into hawks in the winter, because the cuckoos left just as the hawks came. In 1703, a bishop wrote that the swallows all flew to the *moon* for winter!

Since those days, scientists have given us much better explanations. But there are still many mysteries to be solved.

Tundra swans silhouetted against the moon

Overland Trips

Way up north near the top of the earth live the caribou. They are the reindeer of North America. In the summer, the Arctic tundra offers plenty of food for the caribou. But when winter hits, the snow is very deep and hard. The caribou can't dig through it to find food. So, in the fall, the caribou begin to gather together and head south. Small herds join together to make a large herd. Thousands of caribou may travel together.

They may travel from six hundred to eight hundred miles. They head for the timberline, where the tundra gives way to trees. Some herds follow the same trail every year. They often travel single file. In some places, the trail has been worn two feet deep by the many migrations.

When the caribou reach the forest, the temperatures are almost as cold as they are in the Arctic tundra. But in the forest, the snow is not so hard. It can be pushed aside to look for food.

When spring comes, the caribou go back up north. First, they travel north to a safe place to give birth to their calves. In a few weeks, when the calves are strong enough, the herd goes farther north to find more food.

The caribou face many dangers during their migration. A pack of wolves often follows closely behind the herd. They hunt the weak and injured caribou that lag behind. Another danger is flooded rivers. The caribou sometimes follow their trail right into the deep rivers, and young calves often drown.

Some animals make very short overland trips. But their migrations are often just as amazing as the long-distance trips.

Toads are one example. They hibernate during the winter. They dig deep down into the mud or under rocks and sleep until the weather turns warm. Then when spring comes, it is time to breed. So the adult toads begin their migration to the breeding ponds. The trip may be as long as a mile—a long distance for such a small animal.

The males travel first. Then they call for the females to follow. The male giving a call is a funny sight. He inflates his vocal pouch like a balloon.

Generation after generation of toads will follow the same migration route every year. Some routes are hundreds of years old. But in recent years, those routes have led the toads to disaster. More and more roads are being built across migration routes. Thousands of toads have been killed by passing cars. And when so many toads are killed, the animals that feed on the toads are also threatened.

But people are now taking steps to save the toads. Some European countries use road signs that say, "Toad Migratory Crossing." Volunteers on "toad patrol" help by carrying toads safely across the roads. And in Switzerland and England, "toad tunnels" have been built under roads that cross migration routes. With this kind of help, more toads can safely reach their breeding ponds in the spring.

Another small animal that migrates to breed is the red crab. Red crabs live on a small island near Australia called Christmas Island. Every fall, the crabs crawl from the inland rain forests to the shorelines to breed. (Like tadpoles, baby crabs must be born in water.)

The trip to the shore takes nine to eighteen days. There are so many crabs that they look like a moving red carpet! The people on the island keep their doors and windows shut during the migration. They also try not to drive. Crabs often cover the roads. And unlike toads, they can puncture tires with their claws.

The second wave of migration begins when the baby crabs are old enough to crawl out of the ocean. They head for the forests to find food. There may be millions of them! The tiny crabs are only one-fifth of an inch across. They can crawl under doors and through windows. They may turn up anywhere!

Air Travel

While the caribou and red crabs are making their trips overland, thousands of other animals are also on the move high overhead. In spring and fall, the skies are filled with migrating birds and insects. The long-distance champion of them all is a bird called the arctic tern.

The arctic tern may travel up to twenty-two thousand miles round-trip every year. It flies from the Arctic to Antarctica and back. In fact, the arctic tern spends much of its life migrating. Because the tern travels so much, it has to eat a lot of "fast food." When it gets hungry along the way, the tern dives down into the ocean to catch fish.

Red lines show migration routes of arctic tern. Black lines show breeding ranges.

The arctic tern also seems to be a real sun-lover. During the months it lives in the Arctic, the sun shines day and night. Then the tern flies eleven thousand miles south to Antarctica. When it gets there, it again finds twenty-four hour sunshine. So the tern seems to follow the sun.

Another reason the tern flies all the way to Antarctica may be because there is less competition for food there. Not many animals can stand the Antarctic weather — even in the summer.

Another amazing bird is the hummingbird. You may have seen one of these tiny wonders. Like a helicopter, the hummingbird can fly sideways, backwards, straight up, and straight down. The hummingbird is the smallest bird in the world. Yet it migrates hundreds of miles every year.

Perhaps the most amazing is the ruby-throated hummingbird. This bird spends its summers in the northeastern United States. But before cold weather sets in, the hummingbird flies to Mexico or Central America. To get there, it crosses the Gulf of Mexico. That means that this tiny bird must fly at least five hundred miles over water without stopping! The hummingbird beats its wings up to seventy times per second and can reach speeds of up to thirty miles per hour.

Not all air travelers are birds. Monarch butterflies also migrate. In the summer, they live in Canada and throughout the United States. But in the fall, they migrate to California, Florida, or Mexico. Then they fly back north in the spring. The round-trip may be more than three thousand miles! Monarchs have a short life span of only a few months. Those that migrate live just long enough to make one round-trip.

Huge numbers of monarch butterflies migrate each fall. When they reach their destination, they may completely cover the trees. Thousands of monarchs spend the winter in California. And in Mexico, tens of millions of butterflies wait out the cold winter months. Even more amazing, the butterflies often land in the same areas and even on the same trees as the butterflies did the previous winter. They somehow find their way even though they have never been there before!

Locusts are also insects that migrate by flying. But when they migrate, they cause a lot of trouble.

Most migrating locusts live in Africa. They are a kind of grasshopper. When they grow up in an uncrowded place with plenty of food, they develop into normal grasshoppers. But when too many are crowded into an area, they grow up differently. They become brightly colored and grow longer wings than normal grasshoppers. Then they take to the sky in huge swarms looking for food.

Millions of locusts may gather in swarms. People who have seen a locust swarm say it looks like a cloud that "darkens the sun." But the real trouble happens when the locusts land. They eat every growing plant in sight. Scientists are looking for ways to control the swarms and save the farmers' crops.

Sea Cruises

Animals that travel through the air are fairly easy to keep track of. It is much harder to watch animals that migrate through the deep oceans — even when the animals are as large as the California gray whales. These sea giants spend their summers in the cold seas near Alaska. The whales find plenty of food there. But in the fall, they begin a six-thousand-mile trip south to the warm waters of Baja, California. The waters there are warm and shallow — a perfect place for the females to give birth to their calves. The babies don't have enough blubber to survive in the freezing waters up north, even though their average weight is about 1,500 pounds. But they stay warm in the waters of Baja.

Gray whales like to stay near the shore. In December and January, the whales travel very close to the San Diego shore on their way south. People often take whale-watching boat trips to get close to the gentle sea giants.

Another great sea traveler is the Pacific salmon. These fish are born in streams and lakes along the western United States. When they are old enough, they swim downstream to the Pacific Ocean.

When the salmon are old enough to mate and lay eggs, most of them return to the very same stream where they were born—even though they may not have seen the stream for four years! Some of the fish have swum two thousand miles out into the ocean. But they still return to their home stream.

The salmon have to be very strong to swim upstream to their hatching place. They often have to leap up waterfalls and fight rapids. Sometimes bears will stake out a fishing spot near the waterfalls. Many salmon leap right into the jaws of death. But even if the fish make it all the way to their home streams, the trip uses up all their strength. The Pacific salmon live only long enough to breed and lay their eggs. Then they die.

One fish had an especially hard trip. This salmon was born in a hatching tank in California. When it was one year old, the hatchery workers let the fish loose in a stream to swim to the ocean. One year later, the salmon (which had been marked) mysteriously showed up back in the hatchery tank.

In order to get back into the tank, the salmon had to swim 5½ miles up two creeks and through storm sewers, among other things. The end of the trip was the hardest part. The fish had to swim through a four-inch pipe, jump straight up 2½ feet, and knock off the cap at the top of the pipe!

The fish was named "Indomitable" for its amazing efforts. However, Indomitable was not the only salmon determined to return home. Workers found seventy-two salmon squirming around in the canal below the pipe! But Indomitable was the fish that became famous. A sculpture of Indomitable still stands in front of the hatchery.

There are all kinds of amazing travelers that move through the seas. Green turtles are another example. They can move on land too, but they are much faster in the sea.

Not only are they fast, but they have a great sense of direction, too! Every two or three years, many green turtles find their way from their feeding waters near Brazil to a tiny island 1,400 miles away. It is called Ascension Island. They go there to lay their eggs. It takes an amazing animal to find such a small island in such a huge ocean. Some of the turtles even return each time to the same spot on the beach to nest!

Another animal that can travel on land as well as through the sea is the Emperor penguin. The amazing thing about this animal is that it migrates to a *colder* place in the winter! Emperor penguins travel to the shelf ice around Antarctica to have their babies. The winters there are dark, and the temperature gets as low as seventy degrees below zero!

The penguins swim through icy waters and then march single file for miles over the ice. Sometimes they flop onto their bellies and "tobaggan" over the ice, pushing themselves along with their flippers.

But why do the penguins pick such a cold place to lay their eggs? One reason may be that they are safe from enemies there. Few animals can stand the cold. But still, it's a difficult place to hatch an egg. The parents have to keep the egg off the ice. The father rests the egg on the tops of his feet. His stomach sags over the egg to keep it warm. It takes about two months for the egg to hatch. Meanwhile, the mother goes to the sea to find food for the family.

How Do They Do It?

Now we have seen where many animals migrate. But how do they know where to go? This is still one of the greatest mysteries of migration. Scientists don't know all the answers. But they have found some clues as to how animals find their way.

Some animals have very good eyesight. They look for familiar landmarks along their way to keep them on track. The arctic terns may use their eyesight to fly from the top to the bottom of the earth. They probably find their way by following the coastlines of North and South America.

Strange as it sounds, some animals use their noses to guide them! Remember the salmon that return to their home streams to spawn? Well, scientists believe that the salmon "smell their way home." Every stream has different chemicals in it that give it a special smell. The salmon swim up the coast until they find that special smell.

Many animals use the sun or stars to keep on course. In experiments where birds have been taken far from their normal migration route, they have found their way back. Scientists believe the birds found the right direction by looking at the position of the sun or stars. You may have heard of sailors doing the same thing to guide their ships across the ocean.

Many people have long believed that, in addition to the sense of sight and the sense of smell, animals have a mysterious "sixth sense" that guides them. Now scientists may have a clue as to how that sixth sense works. They have found that pigeons have a tiny bit of something called magnetite in their heads. They have found traces of magnetite in other animals too, even monarch butterflies.

Magnetite is a magnetic mineral. How does it help animals migrate? Well, a compass uses a magnet to show which way is north. In the same way, magnetite may act as a "built-in compass" for certain animals. But scientists don't yet understand how animals use this compass.

No matter how many discoveries scientists have made, it still seems a miracle that a butterfly can find one special grove of trees over a thousand miles away.

Tracking the Travelers

We may not always know *how* animals get where they're going. But we do know a lot about *where* animals migrate. How have we learned so much? Scientists have found many ways of studying the travels of animals.

One way is to tag the animals. All over the world, millions of birds are banded. That means that people fasten a very light band around one leg of the bird. That way, they can identify the bird when they see it again. If you look very closely, you may find a banded bird in your neighborhood. Even butterflies can be marked with small paper tags on their wings.

Sometimes scientists attach small radio transmitters to animals. The transmitters send out radio signals so the scientists always know where the animals are.

Researcher with banded sanderling

The Risks Along the Way

Animals migrate to survive. But they face many dangers throughout their trips. Some of the risks are natural, such as the wolves that follow the caribou and the bears that fish for salmon. But many of the risks are caused by man. Migrating birds often crash into tall buildings. Many fish die when they swim into polluted waters. And, of course, there are always the hunters who wait with their rifles for flocks of geese to pass by on their way south.

But if animals did not migrate, many more would die from cold or starvation or predators. For that reason, all over the world, animals are on the move.

INDEX

butterflies, monarch, 24, 42

caribou, 8, 10

crabs, red, 16

hummingbirds, ruby-throated, 22

Indomitable the salmon, 32

locusts, 26

magnetite, 42

migration (defined), 4

navigation, 38, 40, 42

penguins, Emperor, 36

pigeons, 42

risks, 46

salmon, Pacific, 30, 32, 40

terns, arctic, 18, 20, 38

toads, 12, 14

tracking animals, 44

turtles, green, 34

whales, California gray, 28